TEACHING

AGAINST THE TIDE

7 Principles For Succeeding In

A 'Challenging' School.

Matthew Greenslade

Copyright © MATTHEW GREENSLADE

Disclaimer

To respect the privacy of my friends and colleagues who may not want to be publicly recognised, I have altered specific personal details. To maintain child safeguarding practise, I have changed information that might identify any individuals, such as names, gender or appearance.

ABOUT THE AUTHOR

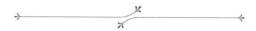

Matthew is a Teach First ambassador and Head of Department. After graduating from Cardiff University with 1st class honours, he joined the Teach First Leadership Development Programme. During his three years in teaching, he has held two leadership positions, the first being awarded during his NQT year. He is now on course to complete an educational leadership MA through the University of Manchester. Much of his practise and research surrounds closing the attainment gap between the most and least advantaged school pupils across the UK.

TABLE OF CONTENTS

About The Author iii

Introduction: Why Have I Written This Guide? 1

What Is A 'Challenging' School? 4

Introducing The Steadfast Seven 8

Section 1: Set Strong Foundations 10

Section 2: Pre-Empt Behaviour.. 24

Section 3: Identify Key Learner Personalities................. 44

Section 4: Plan Smart... 53

Section 5 Know Your Limits 63

Section 6: Know Your Community 76

Section 7: Tackle Extreme Scenarios 85

Concluding Thoughts 98

INTRODUCTION: WHY HAVE I
WRITTEN THIS GUIDE?

This guide is designed to help teachers navigate the daily obstacles that teaching in a 'challenging' school presents. I aim to express my school experience through a series of anecdotes. Each of these stories taught me a different lesson, and I am hoping to pass that knowledge on to you. If you are a trainee teacher, NQT, or teaching in a 'challenging' school for the first time, then this guide is for you.

So, who am I?

I don't recall considering teaching as a career option much before my second year at Cardiff University. It was towards the end of my penultimate year that I started volunteering for the Royal Geographical Society. I enjoyed speaking to pupils across South Wales about Geography, and thus decided that perhaps teaching was a good route to take. I was eventually sold on applying to Teach First through their vision statement.

'No child's educational success should be limited by their socio-economic background'

This struck a chord with me, having never considered the stable platform that my educational experience had provided me with. I did not attend a private or grammar school, but I was educated in a secondary school with an excellent reputation. In hindsight, my experience teaching pupils from a disadvantaged community has made me realise exactly how lucky I was. I was then determined to use the education that I had as a means to provide better experiences for disadvantaged pupils across the UK.

Teach First placed me at a school in the North West of England. Initially, the thought of teaching in a classroom on my own terrified me. Every trainee teacher hears the horror stories of chairs being thrown at teachers and metal detectors in school entrances (often myths in reality), and I will admit that I shared the same fears. During my first year of teaching, I witnessed every form of bad behaviour, abuse and defiance possible. I also laughed more than ever before, and encountered some amazing young people I will never forget. If there is one thing that I hope you take from this guide, it is that children, no matter how tough, how rude or how threatening, are just children. Poor behaviour is very rarely personal. It is how you manage these relationships that mould you as a successful teacher.

At the end of my NQT year, I was promoted to lead geography teacher in the school. The role granted me more control over the department, and I quickly began to focus on the curriculum. I now hold my the position of head of geography at another school with a high proportion of disadvantaged pupils.

Issues, such as behaviour, are debated amongst educators with the key question often being: who is responsible for behaviour? It is inevitable that as a new teacher you will need to develop strategies for dealing with issues such as behaviour regardless of the strategy your school adopts.

However, before we begin, we must discuss the title of this guide. What exactly is a 'challenging' school?

WHAT IS A 'CHALLENGING' SCHOOL?

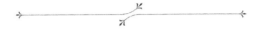

The term 'challenging school' is used by multiple stake-holders. It transcends education and is used in politics, the media, and in everyday conversation. Throughout my time as a teacher, I have heard these schools also referred to as 'tough', 'rough', 'difficult', and even 'failing'. The reputation that these schools hold is not always positive. Friends and family may believe certain stereotypes of what happens within the walls of the school. This guide is not an academic piece of writing, so I am not going to delve into the intricacies of where the term 'challenging' originates, or what it officially includes. Broadly speaking, a school could be 'challenging' if it encompasses one or more of the following statements:

- Below average exam results or progress 8 score[1].
- High proportion of pupils from a disadvantaged background (Pupil Premium, Free school meals).
- High proportion of pupils with Special Educational Needs (SEN).
- Ofsted inadequate or requires improvement.

The term 'challenging' refers to the notion that teaching in them may be more difficult. You may have noticed by this point that I am inverting the word *challenging.* I do this because all schools are challenging. I do not agree with the notion that some teachers have it easier than others, they just face *different* challenges. The pressure faced by a grammar school teacher is not incomparable with those teaching in an inner-city state school, it is just different. I also invert the word because of the negative connotations of the term. These types of school are not worse to work in, far from it. With the right strategies to curb the challenge, they are in fact extremely rewarding.

---

[1] Progress 8 is a measure used by the Department for Education to assess the progress each pupil makes. A minus progress 8 score Indicates that the pupil is making less progress compared to their peers.

So, what exactly are the challenges that make a school 'challenging'? Again, broadly speaking, they exhibit the following:

- Poor or extreme behaviour of pupils.
- Low aspirations of the community, and its impact on pupil engagement.
- Low starting points of pupils. In particular reading age and literacy.
- Additional social care needs required by pupils.

Unfortunately, I do not have the answers as to how these can be solved. However, what I do have is the experience of starting my career in a 'challenging' school. During my time in this type of school, I learned many lessons the hard way. I have battled and fought my way through poor behaviour, low motivation, and disappointing outcomes. At times, it felt like I was teaching against the tide. I had my vision in sight, but the path towards reaching it was fraught with the aforementioned challenges. How could I become a successful teacher if my class were swimming in the opposite direction to me. It was draining and at times disheartening. However, during that time, I learnt strategies that made those challenges far smaller.

I forged relationships with pupils' others were terrified of, and I am thoroughly thankful to all the young people that have made my job interesting and exciting. The pupils that provide the 'challenge' often have home lives I could not imagine existing in a country as developed as the UK. As I state later in the book, children are just children. Wearing a hoody and riding a BMX does not change that. In every 'challenging' school you will find children fascinated to learn about your experiences and eager to start making their own. The secret is unlocking the enthusiasm by dealing with the aforementioned challenges. In doing so, pupils from all backgrounds can access an education of a high standard.

The guide focusses on the challenges presented by working in a school with a high proportion of disadvantaged pupils. The strategies are however applicable to any setting. The methods are the result of my own experiences, and thus are not guaranteed to work every time. They should, however, make working in a 'challenging school' that little bit easier.

INTRODUCING THE STEADFAST SEVEN

Throughout this guide, I will refer to each principle of what I call the 'steadfast seven'. These are the seven broad categories which I deem the most reliable aspects of my teaching. They are a culmination of every mistake and lesson I have learnt in education. The following sections will provide information on each one. I argue that all seven need to act in unison for one to truly succeed in a 'challenging' school.

Set strong foundations

Pre-empt behaviour

Identify key personalities

Plan smart

Know your limits

Know the community

Tackle Extreme Scenarios

SECTION 1: SET STRONG FOUNDATIONS

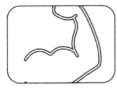

Show Control

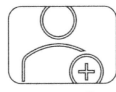

Know your allies

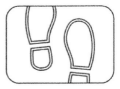

Follow up
consequence

Expectations are
everything

Every teacher is unique. The way your personality shines through in the classroom is what will make the pupils love and respect you. While styles differ, my experience of dealing with challenging classes has made me realise that some traits are vital. Foundations are the core traits that guide how to act in the classroom. Think of them as the vital components needed, from which you then add in advanced behaviour management, planning and actual teaching. I refer to them as non-negotiable since, without them, the 'challenges' become more difficult.

After watching new teachers, it is often clear what foundations they have set. For some, the foundations are rock solid, and the teacher progresses their classroom management extremely quickly. For others, the foundations are weaker and thus new skills are less effective. I have tried to come up with a list of what I consider non-negotiable aspects of my teaching persona. Each serves a distinctly different area, but at its core these are the things that I believe need to be done from day 1.

Non-Negotiable 1: You are in control. Show it.

When I first entered the classroom, it felt surreal. I had just left university and suddenly I had 30 year 8 pupils staring at me. I fumbled around with my seating plan and tried to get the pupils to sit down in their allocated seat. I expected resistance (see behaviour section on 'no') but did not receive any. Five minutes into the lesson, a pupil asked me if they could move seat; they were sat across the classroom from their friends. I double-checked that it was not a more legitimate excuse such as not being able to see the board. To try and show authority, I said no. In reality, I had very little confidence in my ability to stand up for the decisions I had made. Two minutes later, the pupil asked me again. I said no. Two minutes later, she asked again. This time I said yes. What do you think happened next? Suddenly, I had half the class asking to move seats. They had sensed weakness, and now they were going to exploit it. I tried to contain the situation with some authority, but eventually around 6 pupils moved seats (with my permission). My seating plan was in tatters. I had lost control because I had not been able to stand by my decision and have the confidence that I was the one in control. So how should I have dealt with the situation? I could have done it more successfully in a number of ways:

- *'I'm sorry but nobody is moving seats until I review the plan, if it is something serious then please speak to me at the end of the lesson'.*

- *Thank you for raising your concern, if it is serious I will discuss it with you at lunch'.*

By responding in a clear, precise manner, it shows that you are in control of the situation. Things will be changed on your terms, not theirs. This scenario applies to other situations such as asking to go to the toilet or a pupil requesting to leave the classroom for a suspicious reason.

Non-negotiable 2: Know your allies

Standing in front of a challenging class can be daunting. It can also feel lonely. There will be times where a pupil pushes you to the point where you no longer know what to do or how to act. The tip is to always remember that you are not alone, you have 'allies' at your disposal.

Ally 1: School procedure

This may sound obvious, and it is. However, myself and others in my position have started at new schools and not truly understood the systems in place to support staff. It is vital that you do the following:

1. Study the school behaviour policy, and ensure you apply it visually and consistently.

2. Know which member of staff is responsible for whole school behaviour, and each year group.

Let's consider a scenario where school X has the following behaviour policy. A pupil is given three warnings before being 'buddied' to another classroom.

Teacher A follows the system, verbally condemning the pupil's behaviour several times. The pupil is then buddied.

Teacher B does not follow the system. They have lost track of how many warnings have been given, and in their need to remove the pupil they are 'buddied'.

Teacher C follows the system. They write each warning clearly on the board. On the third warning, the pupil is 'buddied'.

It should be clear that the most successful teacher was C. It is very easy to become teacher B when flustered and in the moment. It is equally easy to become teacher A when you are in the swing of the lesson. Teacher A is correct in condemning the pupil and attempting to follow the system. However, by only offering verbal warnings the pupil is not visually seeing the build-up of consequences. This makes it difficult to process and may lead to further misbehaviour. By applying the warnings visually through a name on the board, the pupil is constantly aware that the teacher is following the policy, and thus has no rhetoric to argue the teacher's decision. The same cannot be said for teachers A and B.

Do not fall into the trap of applying policy differently to other members of staff. The more consistent you are with other more experienced teachers, the more the pupils will follow the behaviour policy in your classroom. What is also important is knowing who to speak to. In a situation where a pupil has been completely out of order, or you require support in the classroom, it is vital you know where to locate it. This usually means making yourself aware of who leads each year group for example. Understanding that Mr. Charmers is the head of year 8 makes it far easier to report the rude comments made by a pupil.

Ally 2: Do not fear parents

One of the biggest fears I had in my first year of teaching was calling home. For me, the idea of speaking to strangers about how their son had misbehaved filled me with anxiety. As such, I called home perhaps twice in my first 6 months of teaching. However, I soon learnt to use it as a valuable weapon in my arsenal. I am now in constant contact with parents and carers. If a pupil knows you are willing to speak to home, for both positive and negative reasons, they are far more likely to complete work you have set for them. Remember, you are in control. Forging positive relationships with parents can completely change the relationship you have with pupils. Do not fear it, use it to your advantage. I will give you an example. One pupil in my class was a thorn in my side. He would disrupt my lessons, complete little work and on occasion turn up late. Initially, I resisted phoning home. He was disruptive, but equally he wasn't rude or disrespectful. Maybe it wasn't worth contacting his parents? As his behaviour continued, in the end, I decided to call his mum. The conversation went smoother than expected. She agreed that he was acting poorly, and that if things continued she would take his Xbox away from him. In the next lesson, nothing obvious had changed. I wasn't certain that he had even spoken to his mum. On the first sign of disruption, I just replied 'Xbox'. Not a peep for the rest of the lesson.

Not all phone calls home have been this successful, but many have. I have had phone calls where out of fear I have been too nice, and thus not got my point across. I have called while still wound up by an issue, and ended up coming across poorly to parents. If I could collate some advice it would be this.

1. Start every call with a positive. Coming across negative from the start can harm your relationship with home.
2. Ensure you make your point clear. Do not sugar coat an issue if it is disrupting the pupils own learning, or the learning of others.
3. Focus on the fact that you are calling because you want the best for their child. It is hard to argue this.
4. 'Cool off' before making any calls. A situation may have wound you up, DO NOT unload on a pupils parents.

It is important to note at this point that in 'challenging' schools, there will be a higher proportion of pupils who do not have the home life to facilitate this strategy. For example, pupils may live with care workers or older siblings. There may be a contact number for mum, but the reality is she works 12-hour shifts every day. In a similar fashion, there may be a contact number for dad, but he has substance abuse issues so rarely answers. In this situation, your school will make this clear in some way. This may be a note on the register or an email sent to staff. Use the information compassionately, but do not completely discard the plan to 'call home'. I would advise speaking to the relevant pastoral leader. They will have a plan in place or a process to follow.

Non-Negotiable 3: Follow up every single consequence.

I discovered the importance of this trait when speaking to a year 8 pupil in my form class one morning. The pupil was in and out of isolation for various misdemeanours, but by all accounts, was a very reasonable and bright young lady. We would often discuss her behaviour with different teachers, and as a relatively inexperienced member of staff I was fascinated at why she respected some and not others. One comment she made stuck with me. This is how the conversation went:

Me: Why were you asked to leave English?

Pupil: Miss kept shouting at me for not doing the work

Me: So, are you going to go back and complete it later?

Pupil: No, she never remembers.

Me: Oh, has she spoken to your mum?

Pupil: No. She says she will but never does, so I'm off the hook!

At this point it is very clear the pupil knows there is little consequence for her actions, so she will likely continue behaving in the same way. In sympathy with the teacher, in the hectic day it is easy to forget to do things. I have done the same thing. Based on my own experiences the following rules are absolutely vital.

1. <u>Never</u> make empty threats. If you are challenged, you lose authority.
2. Follow up on <u>every</u> consequence. If you have said you will phone home, phone home.
3. If a pupil skips a request to stay after school or at lunch, follow up the next day through the appropriate channels.

If you follow these three rules, you improve your 'control', and make clear to pupils that there are consequences for their actions.

Non-Negotiable 4: Expectations are everything.

You set the bar in terms of what pupils are expected to do in your classroom. The lower your bar, the lower the outcomes for your pupils. The term 'expectation' is often confused with aspiration. I have been at times misinformed that raising expectations referred to issues like inspiring pupils from a disadvantaged background to apply to university. While important, this is not what the term represents. Put simply, I describe expectations using the following question.

What will I accept, and what will I not accept, in my classroom?

For example, a pupil is chewing gum in your lesson. What do you do? I would assume that the answer is black and white. A pupil shouts out a right answer? Do you accept this? What happens if the class is behaving well, but one pupil is writing while you are speaking? The expectations you set for pupils in your classroom determine the answers to these questions. Think back to your own school experience. Do you remember that strict teacher? Mine was Miss Williams. Contrastingly to other subjects, in her biology class I was an angel. I was too scared not to be. In my younger years, I thought it was because she didn't like kids. In reality, the opposite was true. Behaviour in her classroom was impeccable, and her exams results were even more impressive. She was strict, because she knew what she wouldn't accept in her classroom. When somebody did something on this list, she let you know about it. As a result, she was able to create a classroom culture based on values she believed would aid her class. Some education professionals seek to vilify the notion of being 'strict'. I have even heard the term 'draconian' be used. This is an ill-informed view, in my opinion. Strict does not mean being a bully, being rude or too hard on children. It simply means the bar for what constitutes poor behaviour is higher.

Speak to any teacher, they will say they have high expectations. After all, why wouldn't they. Let me give the contrast to Miss Williams. A member of the senior leadership team gives a presentation on expectation. 'At our school, we set the bar sky high' he announces proudly. 'It is these high expectations that make the behaviour in our school so great'. The day after their presentation, a situation arises . A pupil is running in the corridor. In fact, he runs straight past the SLT member. That pupil is going to get an earful, right? Nothing. The teacher carries on walking without acknowledging the situation. Suddenly, that bar is far lower than it was the day before. In fact, every small piece of behaviour that they let go lowers the bar further. The next day a pupil skips a detention and it is not followed up. Over time, the bar is now closer to the floor than the sky.

The first part of section 2 provides more case study examples of when expectations are dropped and how to prevent this from happening. I also include the three classroom expectations I set for pupils.

To summarise the learnings of this section.

To set strong foundations.

1. You are in control and need to clearly display that fact to pupils.
2. Understanding procedures and key staff is vital to success.
3. Always follow up consequence.
4. Expectations are everything.

SECTION 2: PRE-EMPT BEHAVIOUR

 Low level disruption

 Pupils saying 'no'

 Being sworn at

Let's face it. Fears of, or resulting problems from bad behaviour are most likely the reason you are reading this guide. Unfortunately, I do not have the magic red pill to make your fears completely go away. Nor do I have the blue pill to solve every behaviour that pupil's exhibit. What I do have, are some strategies I use in the classroom to deal with the more common examples of challenging behaviour. These strategies do not 'work every time' but have made a real impact on my ability to deal with some of the most challenging pupils. Some are adaptations of methods I have read; others are methods I have seen teachers use successfully, and some are methods I have developed as a result of a specific experience. These behavioural challenges include:

1. Low-level disruption taking over your classroom.
2. When a pupil simply says 'no'.
3. When a pupil swears at you.

'If one more person shouts out, the whole class stays behind'

Much has been written about how to avoid low-level disruption. However, in my experience it is the single biggest problem facing teachers. Behaviour such as pupils swearing or completely refusing to follow instructions is far less frequent. I faced issues of pupils talking over me, shouting out, and trying to disrupt their friends. I have at times felt completely out of control, faced with a class not following my instructions.

These disruptions become the plague of learning, and eventually lead to further behavioural issues. The more disruptions to your lesson, the less pupils are learning. The less they learn, the lower their outcomes. Disruptions must not be accepted, regardless of how 'low level' they are.

As a department head, I have observed lessons where the teacher has proudly spoken about the good behaviour of their class. In some cases, I get to watch a lesson where the teacher is able to deliver the content they have worked so hard on. In others, I watch the teacher trying to get an important point across but is being. Stopped. By. Interruptions. At. Every. Single. Pause.

To me this implies two possibilities:

1. The teacher has not set clear expectations of the class.
2. The teacher has set expectations, but does not follow them.

Does either situation make them a bad teacher? A million times no. It may however be holding them back from achieving what they want from a lesson. It is highly unlikely the teacher has not set expectations. Every teaching book and training course suggests that expectations are vital. But what does that mean? And why do I so often not see them being followed?

So, let's assume it is the latter possibility. The teacher sets expectations at the start of the term. As weeks go by, their expectations drop bit by bit, until they no longer resemble what they set out to be. Usually, one is oblivious to this. After all, they have not set out to lower expectations. Teaching up to 25 lessons a week brings both physical and mental fatigue, and enough problems to fry a supercomputer. I would argue that by not lowering the expectations, the fatigue would be reduced due to less negative interactions during the lesson. Consider the following scenario, which I observed.

Teacher: Right, who can tell me about the different plate boundaries that exist?

Silence. The class does not respond.

Teacher: One begins with a D...

Pupil A: *(Shouts out)* Destructive!

Teacher: Brilliant, well done! And why do you ....

Pupil B *(Shouts out over teacher)*Constructive!

Pupil C *(Shouts out over teacher)* Transform!

Teacher: No shouting out please.

Pupil B: *(shouts out)* but was I right?

Teacher: Yes.

Pupil D: *(shouts out)* Is Mt Snowden a volcano?

Teacher: Right, one more person shouts out, the whole class stays behind.

During that interaction, can you pinpoint where the teacher lowers their expectations? Faced with the silent classroom (which seems to last forever by the way), the teacher accepts the right answer despite the fact that it has been shouted out. This conveys the message to the class that shouting out is okay. Moments later, the teacher quite rightly attempts to challenge the pupil to expand on her knowledge. She is then interrupted not once but twice. Again, both answers are right. Now, the expectations seem to be in place once again, as she asks the pupils to stop shouting out. Can you now spot the next mistake? No sooner have the expectations been raised, but they are lowered again by her answering the pupil asking if she was right. In that situation, the pupil should not have been answered. Simply asked to put her hand up. By answering the request, the message is again relayed to pupils that it is okay to shout out.

The final mistake the teacher makes is threatening a whole class punishment. By this point, they have lost control of pupils putting their hands up. In my experience, punishing an entire class is rarely effective. You are left with the majority of pupils feeling resentful toward you for keeping them. Here is how the teacher should have handled the situation.

Teacher: Right, hands up, who can tell me about the different plate boundaries that exist?

Silence. The class does not respond.

Teacher: One begins with a D...

Pupil A: *(Shouts out)* Destructive!

Teacher: Could we try that again, with your hand up please.

Pupil A stops and then puts their hand up.

Teacher: Yes, go on.

Pupil A: Destructive

Teacher: Fantastic answer, well done. *Pupil A then expands on her answer*

Teacher: Pupil B, well done for waiting with your hand up. Can you share your answer with us?

In my second example, I hope you noticed the subtle changes. Firstly, I ensured I mentioned 'hands up' when I asked the question. This reminds the pupils of my expectations. When pupil A shouts out, despite the answer being right, I ask them to re-try with their hand up. This further reinforces that I expect hands to be raised before they answer. Pupil B has seen how I dealt with pupil A, and thus will likely now have his hand up (unlike scenario 1). To reinforce the expectation further, I praise him for his compliance. This small action makes it visible to the class that following the expectation will result in positive interaction. The lesson can now flow smoothly, without further interruptions. In a difficult class, this can be the difference between a successful and challenging lesson.

This scenario can be applied to other low-level disruptions such as a pupil flicking a pen, trying to talk to a friend, or making silly comments. By setting expectations early, and keeping to them at all costs, you pre-empt the situation and thus prevent 'losing control'. Low-level disruption is disruption, and it must be picked up on. Allowing it to prosper in your classroom hinders your ability to teach, and the pupil's ability to learn. When I start with a new class, I use the following three expectations.

1. If I am talking, you are silent.
2. If your peer is answering or asking a question, you are silent.
3. Treat others in the classroom with respect.

Each time an expectation is not met, regardless of the pupil or circumstance, they are given a warning. This is made clear to the pupils at the start. Sounds obvious, right? In the scenario expectations 1 and 2 are not met. It is that easy. But consider the expectations. A pupil shouts out over me. I do not acknowledge what they say. I refer to expectation 1. They are given a warning. A pupil tries talking to a friend while his peer is reading out her answer. Expectation 2 is in play. They are given a warning. By making these clear to pupils, and holding them accountable, there are no opportunities for them to argue. That way, punishments are seen by pupils as fairer, as despite not being happy it is clear to them why they are being given a detention. If they are given a detention for shouting out when others have also done so, they are far less likely to accept it. Setting expectations at the start of the term and then not referring to them is not effective. If a class is disobeying them, spend time reminding them of the expectations at the start of a lesson. Have the expectations on your classroom wall, ready to refer to during times of conflict. The time lost will be made up tenfold by the reduction in disruption.

To summarise the learnings of this experience.

Set clear expectations and stick to them vigorously.

1. Do not allow quick wins, such as a good answer shouted out, to lower your expectations.
2. If you feel expectations are slipping, take time to re-set them.
3. Avoid whole-class punishment, no matter how appealing it may seem.

What do you mean 'no'?!

At some point during your teaching career you are sure to experience the phenomena that is 'no'. A lesson may be running smoothly. Suddenly you are met with the open defiance that is no. No can take many forms. It can be can refusal to open a book, it can be a refusal to leave a classroom, along with many other potential scenarios. The ability to deal with 'no' will often make or break your relationship with challenging pupils. It also prevents the pupil from undermining your authority by winning the battle. This section will address the two scenarios in which I have experienced 'no' the most, and how I now deal with it effectively.

Scenario 1: The class has entered the classroom and is completing the task on the board. Ellie is not completing the task. In fact, her book is closed. This frustrates you, because she does this <u>every</u> lesson.

Me: Ellie, open your book please.

Ellie: Urgh.

Me: Now please Ellie.

Ellie: No. I just can't be bothered today.

I move my position to stand in front of Ellie's desk.

Me: Ellie I have asked you to open your book.

Ellie: No, I don't care about Geography anyway.

Me: Ellie this is your last chance to open your book or I will send you outside.

Ellie: Send me out then.

I think it is clear from reading that scenario, that the outcome of that conversation was not positive. It did not generate a positive outcome for me, as I had spent time dealing with Ellie that I should have been using to start my lesson more effectively. It was not positive for Ellie either, who by asking to be sent out was now more disengaged than she was prior to walking into the classroom. When analysing my response, I press Ellie four times. I move closer to Ellie. The focus is entirely on her. Imagine yourself being in a room of your peers at a party. You don't really want to be at the party. The DJ presses you for the next song choice, you say you don't know. He asks you again. You say no. He then moves closer; the rooms attention is now entirely on you. 'So, what song is it going to be then?' he asks. You still don't want to answer, perhaps you don't know what a good song would be. Well, he says, if you don't choose then you may as well leave. Nine times out of ten you leave the party (you may have done so far earlier). This is what Ellie may be feeling in the situation.

So, what can be done? After all, Ellie is in the wrong. I was taught three pieces of advice by an assistant headteacher who, as far as I was aware, very rarely had pupils refuse his request. Even the most challenging seemed to somehow do what he said. My colleagues said it was because the pupils knew his senior position in the school. I don't think the position you hold automatically gives you respect. So I asked him. These are the three things he told me.

1. Less is more.
2. Remove the spotlight.
3. Use praise as a weapon.

By less is more, he referred to the amount of interaction I had with pupil refusing instructions. Why keep pressing the pupil? You should instead control when the conversation ends. If a pupil is not following instructions the first or second time, you should not continue. This undermines your authority as they feel that they can ignore your requests. Simply stop after the second time, and take action. The second is to remove the spotlight. Consider my party analogy. Had the DJ given you a few minutes to think of a song, maybe you would have given him one. No harm done. Finally, using praise as a weapon. His argument was that by praising others in the classroom for compliance, Ellie would take note and want to receive praise rather than negativity. Let's re-enact the scenario following the three pieces of advice.

Me: Ellie, open your book please.

Ellie: Urgh.

Me: *(to Ellie)* I'm going to check on 'Pupil Y'. I hope you make the right choice.

Me: Pupil Y has started really well, brilliant.

Me: Pupil W, really good start well done.

Out of the corner of my eye, I can see Ellie slowly open her book.

Me: Ellie has also made a good start.

Consider the scenario. I have taken the spotlight off Ellie. She no longer feels like the attention is on her. My interaction was one quick, precise response. I was able to monitor the rest of the class effectively. Other pupils in the classroom feel more motivated due to the praise I am handing out, as opposed to spending 5 minutes arguing with Ellie to open her book.

Scenario 2: A pupil has dropped a piece of rubbish in the corridor. You have high expectations, so ask them to pick it up. They say no and walk off.

This form of 'no' is slightly different to the previous scenario. It is less personal; the pupil is outside the classroom so they may feel like they have more power. For this scenario, I propose a simple trick. End the sentence with 'thank you'.

Attempt 1: Excuse me, can you pick that litter up please.

Attempt 2: Excuse me, can you pick up that litter please. Thank you.

Try it. I guarantee you deal with this type of situation more effectively. I do not know the science behind the method. Perhaps by saying thank you, it removes the pupil's chance to say no. Perhaps your assumption that they will do the task by saying thank you before its completion appeals to the moral nature of children. Give it a shot.

To summarise the learnings of this experience. If you experience 'no:

1. Remove the spotlight.
2. Use praise as a weapon
3. Use 'thank you' to assume compliance.

'Ho ho ho, you big jolly ****'

In my first year of teaching I lost count of the number of times I was sworn at, or experienced other staff being sworn at. In my second year of teaching, I was sworn at on 5 occasions. In my third year of teaching I was not sworn at once. You get the picture. So, what changed? When reflecting on altercations, I had never considered how my reaction to situations impacted the pupil behaviour that followed.

Take this story, which is unfortunately completely true. It is the final week of school before the Christmas holidays. I am taking the register for my form class which includes several of the known troublemakers in that year group. The pupils are required to read in silence at the start of every form period. One such pupil was late to form every day, rarely read in silence, and had, on more than one occasion, been particularly rude to me and other members of the form. Within 5 minutes of walking into form that morning, this pupil had left after displaying one of the most shocking (if not creative) verbal abuse episodes I have experienced in teaching. This is how the situation unfolded, let's call the pupil Hayden.

Me: Ah, nice of you to join us Hayden.

Hayden: I'm literally only 6 minutes late.

Me: Okay, if you are 6 minutes late for a plane it leaves.

Hayden: This isn't a plane.

Me: Okay, let's start our reading then please.

Hayden proceeds to read. Within one minute, he is whispering to another pupil.

Me: Boys, silent please.

Hayden reads silently for 30 seconds. He then attempts to get the attention of another pupil across the classroom. I approach Hayden and quietly remind him of my expectations. Hayden ignores these, and proceeds to ask the class who was going to the park later.

Me: Okay Hayden, can you stand outside please.

Hayden: Sir, its Christmas, what's the point of reading?

Me: Because it is what I have asked you to do, now stand outside please.

Hayden: That's not very Christmassy.

Me: Last chance, or you will NOT be going on the trip tomorrow.

Hayden: Well **** you then, ho ho ho and Merry Christmas you big jolly ****.

At the end of this altercation I had no control over my emotions. What then proceeded was an argument with the pupil about how he had spoken to me. Never, and I mean never, argue with a pupil. It does not solve anything.

Now, having read about my experience, hopefully you will have picked up on some of the 'red flags' in my way of dealing with Hayden. Let's ignore the fact that I dealt with the issue publicly. Instead, focus on how my words may have triggered the reaction. Obviously frustrated with Hayden being late, I make a sarcastic comment about the timing. Instantly, the pupil has had a negative interaction with me. This is followed by two further negative interactions. Consider how you would react if met with conflict within moments of speaking to your family, friends, or boss. A child is no different. The mistakes do not stop there. The final nail in the coffin is me threatening to remove him from the trip. On the surface, this sanction seems reasonable. It is. Voicing the consequence in that moment, is not. Clearly wound up by the initial conflict and then being asked to leave the classroom, Hayden's temper is on a knife-edge. My threat pushed him off it. In my experience, 'challenging' pupils reach this knife-edge much faster and more frequently than others. Learning to approach interactions, regardless of how frustrating, in a calm and peaceful way will reduce incidents such as being sworn at no end. I must make it clear, that removing Hayden from the trip as a sanction is entirely appropriate. This should be followed up after the event. Just like adults, children need time to calm down after conflict. Adding fuel to the fire only makes situations worse. In addition, this is also an empty threat. I do not have the power to remove him from the trip, and as such, have undermined by authority once more. This situation took nearly 10 minutes to resolve by myself. That is 10 minutes of teaching time lost, only widening the achievement gap in disadvantaged schools.

However, there will be scenarios in which you are unfortunately on the receiving end of verbal abuse. In those situations, it is important to remember the 'strong foundations' mentioned earlier. In that situation, regardless of how it seems you are still in control. Remember that it is imperative that you follow up on this issue. How you do that is your choice. Refer to the 'weapons' I mentioned earlier. They will serve you well here.

To summarise the learnings of this experience.

If a pupil swears at you:

1. Remember and refer to your foundations.
2. Do not engage with debate or argument with the pupil.
3. Reflect on the event. What could you change?
4. Consequence is vital. Ensure it is administered at the right time to avoid further conflict.

SECTION 3: IDENTIFY KEY LEARNER PERSONALITIES

Disruption

	High	Low
High	Group A	Group B
Low	Group C	Group D

Ability

A fantastic book if you get the chance to read, is *'Surrounded by Idiots'* by Thomas Erikson. In his book, he attempts to explain what he believes are the four types of human behaviour. Education has followed similar attempts to classify learners. The Horsworth Quadrant looks to use scenarios to suggest how best to intervene in pupils learning. For example, a learner can be putting in high effort but making low progress or putting in high effort and making high progress. In theory, this can then be used for the teacher to implement specific strategies for pupils. In a rather crude fashion, I propose a similar model looking at what I call a 'key learner personality'. Please ignore the obvious inaccuracies of this model. It does not cater for every special education need. It does not encompass every single ability level of a pupil. It also cannot be used to replace the knowledge and relationship that you hold with specific pupils.

However, when dealing with issues, I started to notice clear patterns in behaviour. These patterns were not done on the lines of gender or economic status. They simply came from my own observations. I argue, that at a basic level, there are four 'key learner personalities' that could pose different challenges.

Level of Disruption

	High	Low
High	**Group A** • High potential for confrontation • Underachieving • Finishes work quickly • Disruptive to others	**Group B** • Completes work without persuasion • Rarely engages in discussion • Rarely asks for help
Low	**Group C** • High confrontation • Disruptive to others • Requires more teacher support • Requires scaffolding for tasks	**Group D** • Requires motivation to attempt work • Rarely engages in discussion • Often goes unnoticed in lessons

Academic Ability (vertical axis label)

Take a moment to process the chart. I use my knowledge of these groups to supplement the lessons learnt from the behaviour chapter. I will now offer a further description of each group and provide specific solutions for each.

Group A: Disruptive, High Ability

Pupils in this group will undoubtedly become some of your favourites to teach. They are clever, sometimes too clever for their own good. They also have an electric personality. They will crack a wicked smile in your direction, and once you have earnt their respect, they will always say hello wherever you see you in school. They are also incredibly frustrating. Despite their intelligence, they are usually underperforming. Moreover, they can have a destabilising impact on your classroom if left unchecked.

Features of group A pupils:

- Will often tell you if they think you are wrong.
- A clear optimist. 'My grade will be higher when we reach the exam'.
- When engaged, will produce exceptional work. This is not consistent.
- Engage in high levels of low-level disruption.

Strategies to manage this group effectively

- Group A pupils enjoy being presented with problems that need solving – create scenarios and let them apply their knowledge. Simple worksheets are too basic and will cause them to lose attention and begin to distract others.
- Target group A pupils with challenging questions that require them to think. This allows them to speak out loud in a constructive way (as opposed to looking for distractions).

- Raise expectations further. Privately vocalise that you expect more of them than others, as they are the natural leaders in the group. They need to act accordingly.

Group B: Passive, High Ability

In a sense, this group typifies the typical high school 'nerd'. Far quieter than their group A and C counterparts, B's tend to work independently and rarely engage in classroom discussion. Their high ability paired with high work rate means the work they produce is consistently excellent. However, this group is criminally overlooked. On many occasions I have felt guilty about not being able to praise an individual, due to a group A or C taking up more of my time.

Features of group B pupils:

- Rarely seek attention.
- Rarely ask for help, making it difficult for them to improve during the lesson.
- Sometimes resist challenge after completing classwork.
- Will rarely engage in discussion, unless prompted.

Strategies to manage this group effectively

- This group sometimes struggles to receive praise during the lesson. A positive phone call home can have a huge impact on this group's confidence, and relationship with you.
- Include non-negotiable extension tasks for this group. They will usually finish work, and this ensures that they can access challenge without 'asking'.
- Offer out of classroom opportunities to extend learning. These can include subject clubs, or high achievers workgroups. You will see their personality come out more in this setting.

Group C: Disruptive, Low ability

This group is usually the most challenging for new teachers. Disruptive, but lacking the cognitive maturity of group A, pupils in this category make up the majority of 'troublesome' pupils in 'challenging' schools. Likely to make a crude joke to the class, this pupil is often disengaged due to an inability to access the work provided. On one occasion I battled and battled with a group C pupil, none of my strategies at the time seemed to work. That is until I sat down with the pupil to discuss the work. Quite simply, they couldn't start the paragraph they needed to write.

Features of group C pupils:

- Highly disruptive.
- Frequent use of bad language and rude jokes/comments.
- Require high levels of 1-1 support from the teacher.
- Disengage when high levels of reading or writing is involved.

Strategies to manage this group effectively

- Give group C access to clear success criteria so they know precisely what to do in order to be successful. This avoids the excuse to get distracted.
- Group C responds particularly well to verbal praise. Look for 'excuses' to praise the work they are producing.
- Use a timer for tasks. Give the pupils set timeframes to complete a task. Group C pupils lose interest quickly, this aids concentration.

Group D: Passive, Low ability

In my experience, this is the hardest group to deal with. They are the type of pupil who will go unnoticed all lesson, and leave having only written the date and title. Incredibly hard to motivate, these pupils may often have their heads on the desk or even fall asleep during the lesson. Checking in on their learning will usually be met with a meek response, usually saying they are fine or that things are okay. The thought of speaking in front of the class is daunting for this group, and they lack the motivation to answer questions unless directly asked.

Features of group D pupils:

- Appear engaged due to avoiding the distractions of A's and C's.
- Often produce low quality work, with gaps missing.
- Find opening books and starting tasks difficult.
- Extremely low motivation.

Strategies to manage this group effectively

- Use low stake tasks and questions as these can build confidence and success for group D pupils.

- Give group D pupils simple step-by-step instructions that they can refer back to throughout the activity. This places a degree of ownership on the learner and reduces the 'effort' required to complete the task.

- Group D pupils respond well to written praise. Seeing praise written in books or on work usually leads to an increase in work in future lessons. Praise improvements as well as full completion.

To summarise the learnings of this chapter. If you encounter a pupil who is proving difficult

1. Pupils are unique but display common characteristics.
2. Use the features of each group to determine a pupils 'learning personality'.
3. Try using a method specifically designed for that personality.

SECTION 4: PLAN SMART

 Activities do not make a lesson 'fun'

 Maintain work life balance

 Avoid the myth of differentiation

My views in this chapter could be seen as somewhat controversial, in that they contradict what (some) trainee teacher programs promote. In reality, they are the lessons I learnt the hard way. During my first year teaching, I often sacrificed my work-life balance to produce a lesson that was *surely* going to engage 8, set 4 on Thursday afternoon. Education is unique in the sense that every teacher seems to have a different opinion on how pupils learn and succeed best (perhaps I am now a part of that phenomenon). Cutting through the noise is difficult for new teachers.

As you will learn in this chapter, there is a limit to what you can do in advance. I have had lessons I thought were excellent fail miserably, and have used tasks on a whim that have proven hugely successful. The mistakes I often see new teachers making are as follows:

- The narrative that 'lessons need to be fun'.

- Losing the work-life balance due to lesson planning.

- Misunderstanding differentiation.

'It's taken me two hours, but the kids are going to LOVE this lesson'

We have all been there. You stay up late at night trying to plan the 'perfect' lesson for *that* class who just don't seem to listen to you. This time, you are sure they will. To teach the reasons for the outbreak of World War 1, you have divided up the information into 6 groups. Each group will complete a card sort, read a source, and then prepare feedback to the rest of the class. You spend a further 30 minutes cutting up the card sort and placing it all into a neat plastic wallet. 10.45 pm. Job done. The day of reckoning arrives. The class line up following their normal routine and enter the classroom. You split the groups into 6. Chaos. In group 1, Alex does all the work while the others discuss football manager. When group 3 are asked to feedback to the class, they offer a vague answer. It doesn't matter, half the class aren't listening to him, never mind writing it down. The majority of pupils leave the lesson not knowing their triple alliance from their triple entente. I argue that 'gimmicky' lessons, for the most part, provide little benefit for pupils.

One of my favourite stories relating to this issue was a lesson taught by a fellow Teach First participant. For the geographers reading this book, he was attempting to teach global atmospheric circulation, a notoriously difficult topic. To engage the pupils and make the lesson 'fun', he decided to buy pumpkins (the lesson was around Halloween time). Each pupil was to work in pairs to draw the model on the side of the pumpkin. This, he hoped, would make them enjoy what would otherwise be a difficult and bland topic. The lesson ended and he reflected on it. In his own words, it was a disaster. The next lesson not one pupil could explain global atmospheric circulation. He had to reteach the concept. So why did this lesson fail? One reason was that he based the lesson around an activity not the actual concept. This meant that he was not sure what he wanted the pupils to gain from the lesson. Secondly, it failed because some pupils spent too much time focussing on how to draw on the pumpkin. This is time they could have been focussing on understanding the concept. The final reason it failed, is because some pupils didn't have the base knowledge required to start the task. Understanding global atmospheric circulation is one thing, knowing how to draw it on the side of a pumpkin is another. Would you have been able to attempt the task?

At the heart of his lesson, the teacher wanted it to be fun. The aim of all teachers is that lessons should be fun. It is important not to confuse enjoyment through learning with enjoyment through play. I believe that pupils both enjoy and benefit from lessons when they are actually learning. During my first year of teaching, to ensure this was the case, I focused on 4 main questions. In doing so, I streamlined my planning process. Before attempting carousel activities, or elaborate mysteries, I considered what impact they would have on pupils actually learning. I ask myself four questions.

1.) What is the core function of this lesson?
2.) What do I expect pupils to leave knowing?
3.) How will I ensure pupils reach this point?
4.) Are the activities manageable?

So, how could the teacher have used these to improve their 'pumpkin' lesson. The core function of the lesson is for pupils to understand global atmospheric circulation. I would therefore expect them to leave knowing that warm air is moved from the equator to the poles by a series of circulation models. Now that this is clear, I could then plan appropriate activities which ensure that the pupils clearly met this goal. Perhaps I would follow the *'I do, we do, you'* do method. Full disclaimer, I did not invent this method. Put simply, I would model the process of global atmospheric circulation to the class through direct instruction. I would then work through the model with the class, per-haps hiding certain labels or information for them to com-plete alongside me. When confident that they understand the process, I would then give them a task to complete in-dependently. This would result in more pupils being able to access the work. If after the 'we do' stage you are not confident in pupils knowledge, simply repeat steps 1 and 2.

Alongside the four aspects of each lesson, I would also consider whether the activities were manageable. This is twofold. Firstly, I mean manageable for me in terms of workload. I always refer to the economic principle of the law of diminishing returns. Applied to education, the law argues that there is a tipping point, where effort put into a lesson does not result in better pupil outcomes. It also influences a teachers work life balance. As a general rule of thumb, a 50 minutes lesson should take a maximum of 50 minutes to complete. I also refer to manageability in terms of pupils. If you have a class with a number of group A and C pupils, getting them out of their seats is a recipe for disaster. Likewise, promoting group work with a num-ber of different group B pupils will likely lead to only one from each group completing the work. That is not to say that these methods should be avoided altogether. I am simply suggesting that the basics are right first, before they are implemented. The lesson should be planned based on knowledge, not to shoehorn in a fun looking activity. Remember, not every lesson has to be 'outstanding'. Sometimes okay is good enough.

'Pupil A has this worksheet; pupil B has this worksheet. Pupil C is doing this.'

Differentiation. A term that frustrates and confuses me in equal measure. In layman's terms, differentiation means providing different avenues for different pupils, so all can learn effectively. If you have already started your training or currently work in a school, no doubt you know all about this term. It seems as if every teacher has, at some point, been told different things about what differentiation is. I have received advice that effective differentiation means providing different worksheets for the different ability levels in a class. As such, I spent much of my first year teaching desperately trying to cater to every pupil in the class. I have also received lesson observation feedback suggesting that I should include clear differentiation in the form of offering different card sort information for certain pupil groups. Consider the long-term impacts of differentiation in this form. If pupil A follows a 'dumbed down' curriculum in the form of differentiation, then by year 11 how much further behind is he then pupil B who has followed the full scheme of work? Let's say pupil A is from a disadvantaged background and pupil B is not. Is their education equal? I like to visualise this concept as a bar.

By dumbing down my content, I am allowing pupils to fall below the knowledge I expect all pupils to know. Does this benefit the pupils in my class? They are heading for the same endpoint after all. I thus argue that this should be rejected; it does not help you or your pupils to succeed. I do, however, support the notion of challenge activities. As previously mentioned, challenge is essential for pupil groups A and B. They allow them to prosper beyond the expected level. They do not hinder others in the class from reaching the expected point.

To avoid this trap, I refer to differentiation by scaffolding. This method carefully places 'scaffolds' within the lesson to ensure that pupils reach the same end point. Consider the following lesson. At the end of the lesson, I want pupil to leave with a greater knowledge of how to answer a 9 mark exam style questions. It is a mixed ability group, some pupils are predicted grade 7's while others are pre-dicted 2's. However, I am not going to provide 'easier' exam questions or dumb down the answers that I require. Instead, I am going to provide scaffolds for the different groups. For ease, I will break them down into the 4 'key leaner personalities'.

Group A+B	Group C+D
Give success criteria for high level answers	Given essay structure strip to help get started

To challenge the higher ability pupils, I give the success cri-teria for how to achieve a high level answer. This provides challenge, and allows them to access the top grades. This can clearly be presented on a PowerPoint while the pupils write. For groups C and D, rather than change their con-tent, I suggest scaffolding as an effective method to en-sure they keep up with the pace of learning. On a basic level, this may mean providing an essay structure strip for lower ability pupils. A structure strip enables them to see what types of things they should include in their answer, such as an introduction, or a point evidence explain (PEE) paragraph. In that scenario, they would still complete the same essay as the middle and higher ability pupils. The end product will undoubtable be of a lower quality than groups A and B, but it allows pupils to access the task without dumbing it down.

To summarise the learnings of this chapter.
When planning lessons:

- Choose knowledge over activities.
- Respect the law of diminishing returns. Okay is sometimes good enough.
- Avoid using 'dumb down differentiation'. It will impact your outcomes.

SECTION 5 KNOW YOUR LIMITS

 You may not impact every pupil the way you envision

 Timetabling is out of your control

 You influence, but do not set school culture

A strategy for thriving in a 'challenging' school can simply be understanding what is, and is not, in your control. Schools are strange places. Things happen in schools that would not happen in any other workplace or in any other profession. That is something you will learn to love, but in the beginning, it can be very difficult. Schools should always prioritise resources to benefit new or inexperienced teachers, but that is not always the reality.

Teaching in multiple classrooms is a challenge you will no doubt have to face at some point. I argue that things like that are inevitable. You need to take ownership of the factors in your control. There are other things that are out of your control. I believe that a lot of people joining teaching do so to help make a difference. They want to be 'that' teacher that inspires every pupil they meet. Unfortunately, forging good relationships with every pupil is not in your control. Nor it is in any teacher's control. This chapter outlines three areas where your limits may be stretched.

1. Impacting every pupil in the way you want.
2. Timetabling issues.
3. Changing the way pupils think about school.

'I want to be the teacher who inspires the next generation of engineers'.

Entering teaching with a vision or moral purpose is important. You should have an idea of what impression and impact you want to have on pupils. In the introduction to this book, I briefly referred to my vision. There is no right or wrong vision. There is no right or wrong reason to get into teaching. However, sometimes it is important that your vision does not become something that can hold you back. Consider the following statement:

What you can't control: Impacting every pupil in the way you want.

What you can control: Making a meaningful impact on some.

Let's follow the story of Will. Will is a maths teacher, who also teaches some design and technology. He had studied civil engineering at University College London. One Tuesday afternoon at the weekly CPD session, I was paired to work with Will. CPD sessions focus on a teacher's professional development. I forget the topic of the session, probably something about differentiation. Having never previously spoken to Will, and sensing he was an NQT, I asked him why he had got into teaching. After all, I was surprised he was not out designing bridges or new buildings. His response was straightforward. 'I want to be the teacher who inspires the next generation of engineers'. As it turned out, after getting to university he was completely shocked at the socio-economic background of his cohort. From his perspective, up to 90% of the course was middle class. He recalled his own school experience and concluded that the reason he got into engineering was because of a maths teacher who loved using buildings in the lessons. Thus, his reason to join teaching was born. And what an inspiring reason it is. The problem was, Will made it too personal. As the weeks went by, Will was met with opposition. Pupils disrupted his lessons and spoke over him when he promoted his love of engineering. Over time, Will became disillusioned. He considered whether it was time to leave the school or perhaps leave teaching altogether. Another CPD session came around and I decided to check in on Will. He explained the situation to me. I had nothing but sympathy. I arrived into teaching with the mission to use my skills to aid the education of the most disadvantaged pupils, and yet I was met with the same reaction as Will. I gave Will the following three pieces of advice:

1. Not everybody enjoys drawing and numbers. I don't.

2. Providing great lessons will benefit pupils in the long term, even if they don't show it immediately.
3. Focus on the small victories. Do any pupils engage?

I'm not sure Will enjoyed my first comment, after all, drawing and numbers was his bread and butter. I believe the second point speaks for itself. To him, it may appear that he is having little impact on his pupil. The opposite is true. Providing good lessons on a regular basis helps all pupils in the long run. He did however seem to pay particular attention to the third point. I saw the cogs in his brain working. Well he said, pupil A did ask me why skyscrapers don't blow over in strong wind. He had realised that he could have a huge impact on some pupils. This leads me to my lessons from this experience, they are as follows:

- Being a consistent teacher is more than good enough.
- Children are not computers. They will not react in a given way, even when you hope they do.
- Focus on the small positive impacts you are having upon certain pupils.

'Sir, why are we doing Geography in the science block?'

If this segment does not currently apply to you, then great. Hopefully, it never will. Probability suggests otherwise. Schools are facing an increasing number of challenges. Pupil populations are rising while school funding, in real terms, is decreasing. As such, sacrifices have to be made. Teaching outside your classroom is uncomfortable. Even if it is in the room next door it still feels, well, *different*. In my first year of teaching, I had my own classroom. By my third year I taught across the humanities classrooms, in English, and in science. At the start, I resented it. How would the headteacher expect me to teach some very difficult classes if I was constantly moving classroom? It was only as I began my transition into leadership that I changed my opinion. While not ideal, it is sometimes necessary. It was not something I could control. But there were things I could.

What you can't control: Room changes and timetabling.

What you can control: Establishing routine in each scenario.

So, when have I seen this happen? Most commonly, you will have to use the classroom of another teacher in your department. In this scenario, communication is key. My most shocking example came from another Teach First participant who taught in a 'shared learning space'. In reality that means an open classroom slap bang in the middle of the school. She had a terrible experience and never truly learnt how to take control of the space she occupied. Her discomfort with her surroundings put her on edge, and impacted her ability to teach the class. My most extreme experience of teaching outside my comfort of the humanities corridor occurred at the start of my third year of teaching. My year 7 lesson was scheduled to take place in the Science block period 2. The walk to the next classroom was approximately 4 minutes. Before the lesson, I taught in my normal Geography classroom. This is how the first lesson went.

1) I finish lesson 1 on the bell. Packing up the classroom and dismissing pupils takes me a further 3 minutes.
2) I grab the resources for the next lesson and walk to the classroom.
3) I am now 7 minutes into the lesson.
4) It takes me a further 3 minutes to load my PowerPoint. The class is unsettled. Some
5) To hurry the lesson, I dive straight into my starter task. Forgetting to do the register.

6) Flustered, the behaviour for the reminder of the lesson is terrible.

7) I end the lesson, spending 5 minutes tidying the classroom.

8) I walk back to my classroom, with 3 minutes left of break time before my next lesson. Exhausted.

Safe to say, it was not a success. While reading my account, I hope you have noticed things that you could or would have done differently. For starters, I treated both lessons in isolation. Effective planning for lesson 2 in science would require me to factor in the end of lesson 1. Let's not even get started on the fact that my lesson started perhaps 15 minutes later than usual. The behaviour was terrible because my expectations were lower. Out of my classroom and in the circumstance, my foundations crumbled. I did not reach a solution overnight. In fact, I slowly began to find strategies that worked over the course of a term. In the end, the key point was ensuring that wherever I was teaching, a clear routine was in place for pupils.

- I finished lesson 1 with alternate plenaries such as the use of sticky notes and verbal feedback. Books were packed up with 10 minutes remaining rather than at the end. I could then leave on the bell.

- I ensured that pupils in my next lesson knew to line up and wait for me. I spent 25 minutes one lesson practicing the line to get it right.
- I pre-printed the 'do now' and starter tasks on a worksheet. These were handed to pupils as they entered. This bought me time to set up my laptop and do the register.

While this is still not the perfect situation, it allowed the lesson to flow and produce more positive outcomes for pupils. So why have I shared this experience? Understanding how to implement routine is a vital aspect of successful teaching. By taking control of the situation and implementing new routines, behaviour was much improved as I was able to rely on my foundations safe in the knowledge that I was in control.

'Alright Sir, but everybody fails here anyway'

Every school has a 'culture'. You may see school slogans promoting a *'culture of success'* or a *'culture of collaboration'*. Strip away the motto and watch what is happening in the corridors. Watch how the pupils act in the canteen at dinner. Do they line up sensibly? How do they speak to canteen staff? See how they interact with each other, listen to the language that they use in the corridor. Are pupils smiling? Are staff smiling? That is the real culture of the school. So why does this relate to you? Well, some schools have an amazing culture. The pupils treat staff and their peers with respect, and a nice atmosphere exists when you walk through the building. Unfortunately, many don't. It is easy to be bogged down and hindered by whole school culture. However, at the moment, you can't change it.

What you can't control: Whole school culture. The values instilled in all pupils.

What you can control: Classroom culture. What happens in your classroom is yours to control.

This section is written under the assumption that the school culture is somewhat poor. Perhaps pupils regularly swear in the corridors or staff are often treated without respect. There may be poor respect for uniform, and dreadful punctuality of pupils. Perhaps a culture of failure exists, whereby pupils feel like they cannot achieve. Let me make this clear. You contribute to culture, but do not create it. You may influence it, but you cannot change it alone. This again links to expectations. There will be times where the expectations of other staff, or even school leaders do not match your own. Consider this scenario. I once taught a pupil in year 9. By all accounts, he was clearly a group C student. He was confident and at times disruptive. He wasn't however rude. Using the techniques I have previously mentioned in this guide, the pupil was working well in my lesson. One morning I saw the pupil and his friends being very aggressive toward another teacher in the school. Now this teacher could handle herself, but I went to support

Nevertheless, upon arriving, the aforementioned pupil told me to 'stay out of it'. Incensed, I requested he speak to me in my classroom immediately. This is how the conversation went.

Me: That was very rude, you know.

Pupil: Sorry sir, I didn't mean it

Me: Thank you for your apology. You have never been rude in my lesson. That felt very out of place. Is everything okay?

Pupil: Yeah, but it wasn't a lesson so it's different.

Me: You should not change your behaviour based on your surroundings.

Pupil: Okay, Sir.

Any guesses what happened only two days later? I see the same pupil be rude to another member of staff in the same way. This infuriated me and I brought up the issue with a more senior colleague. The pupil was sanctioned appropriately. What happens a week later? It happens again. Yet alongside this, the pupil was behaving impeccably inside my classroom. I was confused. He had faced consequence but was still portraying the same behaviour. This is where school culture comes in. This pupil was not an isolated incident. In fact, his reaction to me and others was a carbon copy of the way other pupils acted in a similar situation. Yet, for some reason I couldn't let it go. It ate away at me. Eventually I realised that I couldn't control everything. Perhaps I had wrongly assumed that my expectations were parallel to others. Maybe the underlying expectations from staff, including myself, outside the classroom meant that this was a normal reaction.

Nonetheless, this is what I learnt:

- For a teacher, behaviour in the classroom is the most vital aspect.
- Whole school culture is set by policy and procedure. This is set by senior leadership and the headteacher.

- Do not stop trying because others have. Keep expectations high wherever you are in the school.

To summarise the learnings of this chapter:

- Focus on small victories, not unrealistic goals. You will not reach them overnight.
- You can control parts of every scenario. Find those things and make sure you do.
- You contribute to culture, but you do not create it.

SECTION 6: KNOW YOUR COMMUNITY

 Dealing with life as an 'outsider'

 Developing relationships outside the classroom

 Building local context into your teaching

Hopefully by this point in the guide you are now considering using some of the strategies in your classroom. This section extends far beyond the classroom. Working in a 'challenging' school often means working in an area of high socio-economic deprivation. These areas often have a stigma attached to them. For example, certain inner city areas may have a less than sparkling reputation on the outside. When I started teaching, I saw the school's local community as an opportunity. Thinking back to my own school experience, I usually got on with teachers I could relate to. Perhaps they were a fan of the local football team, so I could chat with them about that. Perhaps they knew about a popular takeaway and could relate with the class about the amazing samosas that were on offer. Now unless you were born in the area you teach, you are unlikely to hold this knowledge. So why am I talking about community? Let me explain. There are three experiences that I have had thus far in education relating to the community. They include the following:

1) The notion of being an outsider in the eyes of my pupils.
2) Engaging with school events.
3) Using local knowledge to increase engagement.

'Call yourself a Geography teacher? You don't even know where Seacombe is'

Moving to a new area is challenging. Moving to a new area to teach more challenging still. When I started teaching, the only view I had of the area I taught in was through my car window. I drove the same route every day, rarely stopping to pause and actually look. This is perfectly normal behaviour. It was after a small conversation with some pupils that I realised quite how little I knew about the area. It went something like this:

Me: Alright lads, got anything fun planned for the weekend?

Pupil A: Yeah sir, we are heading down Senny park for a chill.

Me: Oh brill, where is Senny?

Pupil: Call yourself a Geography teacher sir? You don't even know where Seacombe is.

He was right. If I'm being honest, I had no idea where he was talking about. It wasn't the specific area the school was located in. As it turned out it was one of 6 areas that fed into the school. So why is this important? Well, as a new teacher it can be difficult to establish yourself. Gaining any advantage possible is therefore a good move to make.

Based on this experience, this is what I recommend you take the time to do when joining a new school or area.

1) Go for a short walk around the local community. See what the unique character of the place is. See the local landmarks pupils consistently refer to.
2) Head to Google and research the history of the community. It is amazing what you can find.

'Dad, that's my Geography teacher'

One of the best aspects of being a teacher, is that you never know what is coming around the corner. I once taught a pupil, a clear group B. She was a keen student and completed every piece of work I set for her, and more. Being a group B, she was very quiet. She would often give me a smile when I pronounced a word wrong, or laugh in sympathy at my horrendous jokes in the lesson. One morning, she came into my classroom and offered me the chance to buy a ticket for the school show. Initially, I was wary. The show started at around 8 pm midweek. It would be nearly

11 pm by the time I got home. I agreed and handed over £2 for my ticket. I recall arriving at the show with a degree of trepidation, I remembered the 'talent' on offer by my peers when I was in school. As it turned out, I did not need to worry. The evening was amazing. Pupils I taught transformed into dance, song, and drama. Some of the initial performances were amongst the funniest I had seen in a long time. Up next was the pupil from my class who sold me the ticket. Her voice was truly amazing. I had never considered this aspect of her personality before, and it took me aback. So why am I telling you this story? At the time of the show, I knew the pupils I taught and that was about it. Maybe I knew about 35% of the pupils in the school. Well, the next morning I felt like I knew a whole lot more. I started to see the faces of the pupils who had performed their dance piece. It was also refreshing seeing pupils who had, at times, causes issues in my lessons in a different light. This improved my relationship with them and enabled me to teach more effectively. This is my first lesson from the experience; say something to every pupil you see. The morning after the show I did just that. It really doesn't matter what. *How's it going* or *good morning* are fine. But do take the time. In a 'challenging' school, due to the home life and context of the community, sometimes it will be the first meaningful interaction that pupil will

have experienced that day. Do not be discouraged if pupils do not always reply at first. Over time, they will.

In the subsequent year, I attended every show or extra-curricular performance I could. On one occasion, I volunteered to run the ticket table. My job was to greet parents and members of the community and attempt to slog tickets for the raffle. In doing so, I interacted with many families and friends of the local community. I learnt what their jobs were, and I heard first-hand the situation that many of them were in. It was heart-warming and made me feel a part of it. Sometimes pupils would exclaim that I was their geography teacher, others turned up donning football shirts of teams you wouldn't expect. One pupil had the audacity to turn up in a Chelsea shirt once. As it transpired, he had moved to the North West when he was 6 and his father had made certain he did not succumb to the allure of Liverpool or Manchester United. This provided another opportunity to build my relationship with the pupil that would not have previously existed. Following this example is time-consuming, for certain. However, there is no better way to embrace yourself in the community and in school life. Another worthwhile option I could suggest would be to volunteer for more roles such as monitoring dinner ques or the playground. However, I am not going to suggest you do this until you feel comfortable with the school. You deserve time during the day, whenever that may be, to cool off and be away from pupils. If you feel you don't need it, then use the time to your advantage. As such, I recommend the following.

- Take time to submerge yourself in the school and community.
- Interact with every pupil possible, even if you don't teach them.
- Use what you learn to build stronger relationships with pupils.

'Wait, find my house?!'

Prior knowledge is a powerful device. One of the key issues facing disadvantaged pupils is a lack of what OFSTED call *cultural capital*. The theory reads along the lines that a middle-class pupil may progress quicker in French, because he has seen some words used on his skiing holiday to Val-d'Isère. I am not going to suggest how to solve this in a disadvantaged context, as this is something I am yet to fully understand. What is apparent however, is that the same base concept can be applied to pupils to improve engagement. What I mean by this is that lived experiences are powerful. Personalising your teaching to the experiences you are confident pupils have lived is a vital tool to foster engagement.

As a geography teacher, it is difficult to avoid maps. Maps are notoriously boring for pupils who believe Google can show them everything (to some extent, they have a point). I once tried to introduce the concept of layered maps, for example, crime rate in certain communities. I showed pupils a map of London. Tumbleweed. Even the most engaged pupils looked at me with distaste. In the next lesson, I changed tactics. This time, I showed them a map of their local area. The response was completely different. Pupils were eager to find out the crime statistics for their street, their favourite park. *What type of crime happens during the day sir? Why is there more crime in winter than now?* Without realising, the pupils were asking questions to a level I could not have anticipated. So why have I chosen this story? The point is that the pupils felt involved in the learning process. They could relate the experience to their life. Consider the following when teaching in the future. How can you relate teaching to your pupil's lived experience? What links to the community and everyday life can be made to make the content relatable? My story could easily be transferred to other subjects. Using local air pollution in science, calculating the ratio of products used in local hairdressers, or writing gothic fiction about a scary place in the pupil's community for example.

To summarise the learnings of this chapter. To know your community:

1) Spend time exploring and gaining an insight into the community.
2) Use this knowledge to apply context to your pupils.
3) Use lived experiences as a powerful tool for engagement.

SECTION 7: TACKLE EXTREME SCENARIOS

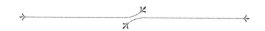

 What happens when nature enters the classroom?

 How to manage 'fights'

 Forgetting your kit

What do I mean by an extreme scenario? These are the things my friends always like to ask me about. They are hell-bent on asking about fights and gangs. I often feel they know little about where I work. Maybe in their mind, I'm actually a prison guard? It all stems back to my introduction; people have misconceived ideas about teaching. However, fights do occur. Fights occur in most schools. They are, however, somewhat rare. Sure, they happen, but the chances of you experiencing one are slim. Slimmer still that one occurs in your classroom. This is not the only extreme scenario that you may experience. The following chapter details some of the more ridiculous things that have happened during my time teaching, and how I have dealt with them. They proceed as follows:

1) When nature enters the classroom.
2) Fight, fight, fight.
3) Forgetting your kit.

'But sir, Charlie has just been mugged off by a seagull'

Nature entering the classroom is a unique experience. The way pupils react to a fly entering the classroom makes you wonder whether they have ever seen one before. Don't even get me started on a wasp. The situations can be highly amusing, but also chaotic depending on the class, time, and situation. I once had a lesson observation completely ruined by a pigeon. This pigeon had decided that my classroom windowsill was the ideal place to sit and watch the world around it. At first it received little attention. Then it flew off and came back for a second time. And then a third. Each time the pigeon returned it received a cheer from the class. Geography was well off the menu today. I closed the blind but failed to recover the lesson. I was mortified. This was my first lesson observation at the school and the star of the show was an old pigeon with a slightly short leg. Over time I learnt to see the funny side, and the kids still remember it to this day. Not ideal when you are trying to make your mark, however.

My favourite (and most testing) interaction with nature came during a year 9 geography lesson. In the middle of teaching my pupils the role of coastal abrasion, we hear a noise. Stay sat down, I tell the class. I peak my head out of the door. 'What is it Sir?' ask my class. I decide the best course of action is to ignore it and carry on teaching. 'Nothing', I tell them. Sadly, my lie was soon to be found out. No sooner had I got the class re-focussed, the huge seagull I had spotted a minute earlier waltzed past my classroom door. Bedlam. 'What should we do sir?' my class asked. I decide to send an email to the site management, informing them of the problem. There were still 30 minutes remaining of the lesson so it would be sorted by the time pupils were back on the corridors. One pupil, let's call him Charlie, wasn't satisfied with my response. 'Don't worry sir', he said confidently. 'I'll sort this'. Before I had a chance to block his exit, Charlie was out on the corridor. Sensing danger, I followed him, urging he come back into the classroom. Charlie was now goading the seagull. Perhaps his strategy was to lure it off the corridor and back to the playground doors it had appeared from. In fairness to Charlie, his plan worked. The seagull started to move toward the exit. What Charlie did not anticipate was that seagulls can fly. The gull spread its wings and started to accelerate down the corridor, knocking Charlie off his feet. I had absolutely no idea what to do next. I decided to send Charlie to first aid, just in case he had been hurt in any way. Back into the classroom I go, ready to move on to the next topic: attrition. My class protested. 'But sir, how can we do Geography now, Charlie has just been mugged off by a seagull'. They were right, no learning would take place today.

Scenarios like this may never happen. My argument is that if they do, fine. The randomness of teaching is what makes the profession great. One off-set lesson will not harm the pupils. Their relationship with you will improve tenfold. There are a few things that should always happen from the teacher's perspective.

1) You need to stay as calm as possible. Pupils feed off your energy.
2) Pupil safety is paramount. ALWAYS follow something up if there has been any potential harm.
3) Sometimes, it is okay for learning to come second.

'Mate, he is going to get banged'

When it comes to fights, I do not want to give poor advice. Nor do I want to scare anybody. They are rare, and when they do happen there are often more experienced teachers ready to intervene. I am in a strange position. I am 6ft 5" and have never been worried about the physical implications of a fight. I have colleagues who feel the complete opposite, and rightly so. As such, I do not have tried and tested strategies on how to intervene. I'm sure there is a wealth of literature discussing what to do, but sadly this is not one. What I will offer however, is my experience of how to 'cool down' tempered situations. As far as I am concerned, most fights happen for the following two reasons:

1) Pupils defending friends or family. Many fights don't involve both of the main aggressors.
2) Factor external to school e.g. an argument continuing from the weekend.

For example. In one scenario, there was anger amongst a group as a result of a text message that had been sent by another pupils' sister. As a result of this text, the group confronted the pupil. A fight broke out. From the outside, the pupil had nothing to do with the issue, it was her sister after all. That didn't seem to matter. In another scenario, a fight broke out after school on the field. The two pupils had never appeared to have any issues, so it felt strange. As it transpired, there had been an argument on the weekend. The two were neighbours and one had taken a joke a bit too far on the walk home from school. So how does this relate to you? I believe that most fights could be prevented by a teacher recognising the precursors. A bit like a volcano eruption, the majority of fights do not happen instantly. There are minor tremors in the build-up.

These include:

- Groups of pupils in heated discussion about something.

- A disruption to your lesson that seems out of place.
- Multiple pupils whispering about the event.
- One or more pupils looking worried or scared.
- One or more pupils visibly angry or sad.

Consider this experience I had:

Midway through break I notice two pupils arguing on the humanities corridor. I sense a fight is about to happen.

Me: Okay guys, what's up?

Pupils: Nothing, Sir.

The pupil argument steps up a notch, other pupils begin to crowd around. One pupil in particular is very wound up, she will struggle to calm down.

In this situation, what would you do next? You can't do nothing, but equally, the chances of immediate mediation are slim. Here are the steps I could have used to help prevent this, or another fight from happening.

- Immediately isolate the more PASSIVE pupil from the situation. They are more likely to listen to your instructions. You could do this in a classroom or send them away completely. Thus, the fight is avoided.
- Remove the crowd. They will not help the situation.
- Ask the more aggressive pupil if there is anybody they would want to speak to. Usually, there is a teacher, or member of pastoral staff they feel comfortable with. It does not have to be you.

By following these steps, there is a chance the argument will diffuse. Do not allow the argument to progress, as you will then have to deal with more conflict. Equally, in this situation the steps may not present themselves. In that situation, you could try the following:

- Ask a pupil to find a certain member of staff e.g. Head of Behaviour.
- Seek support from another staff member in close vicinity.

Your school will offer further information on specific policies, but these are the methods I have used to try and avoid full-blown conflict. They will not always work, but they may help guide you if the situation does arise.

'OMG, it's Lance Armstrong'

The final extreme scenario I wish to discuss is rare, but highly embarrassing. For those of you that went to a school similar to mine, forgetting your PE kit was a cardinal sin. You knew that they would have to have to play rounders in the spare kit which had not been washed for millennia. Perhaps it was too small, or even worse, you were combining with the girls for that lesson. To cut a long story short, it's embarrassing. As I have stated before, teaching is a unique profession. What you do, wear, and say is judged by hundreds of children every single day. It can be highly amusing, but also terrifying. On one occasion, I noticed members of my class giggling, unable to hide their amusement. I remember smiling and asking them what was so funny. 'Nothing sir' they replied, a smile still beaming across their face. As my lesson progressed, I noticed more and more pupils grinning. 'Right, what is it then' I asked. 'I know you aren't this enthusiastic about the industrial revolution'. Up steps Charlie (Seagull Charlie). AVENGERS, ASSEMBLE he shouts. The class burst into hysterics. It transpired that I had chosen a rather colourful pair of socks that morning. Iron man socks to be precise. My class were quick to point out that this was not the first time I had worn such tragic attire. 'It was spiderman last week' one pupil commented. 'At least they aren't odd, they usually are' chirped another. I must admit, I found the situation hilarious. They were right, after all, my socks were dreadful. This situation was very much in my control. However, I have seen examples where the control is somewhat taken away.

A former colleague of mine loved cycling. He loved it that much, he would cycle to work regardless of the weather or time of day. Rather than get his suit dirty, he would leave it in a locked closet in school, then change into his cycling gear. One morning, he was being observed by his university tutor. Everything was going to plan. He arrived at work at the normal time, which would give him 20 minutes to set up the classroom. The problem was, he couldn't open the closet containing his suit. Rather than being in its normal location in his wallet, the key was back at his house. With no opportunity to return home, he had no other options. He then proceeded to teach the entire day in his cycling gear (which by all accounts was a very tight material). He maintains that one of the pupils called him Lance Armstrong. I refrain from making any crude jokes. I tell this story for because it provides an example of when things don't go according to plan. Things like this do unfortunately happen. If your wardrobe malfunctions in a normal office job, no big deal. With all eyes on you, things feel different. I asked him how he managed behaviour that day. He advised that the best thing he did was see the humour in the situation. By making the joke apparent straight away, the pupils could then 'get over it'. If he had failed to acknowledge the situation, I imagine most pupils would be distracted by the tightly dressed elephant in the room.

Another extreme situation in this form is dealing with a technical issue, or worse yet, forgetting a memory stick. Very early in my teaching career, my school suffered a day without the internet. All my lessons were stored on my cloud, and thus I had no way of teaching. Having never faced an issue such as this before, I had no idea what to do. I relied on my PowerPoint and felt useless without it. The behaviour that day was awful, perhaps the worst I have ever experienced. I was terrified at the thought of it happening again. A year or so later, it did. This time, I had forgotten my memory stick (and not backed it up). Only realising I had forgotten it just before the start of school, it was too late to beg for help from my colleagues. So what did I do? I improvised. For some classes, I taught a 'reflection' lesson. The pupils needed to go back through their books and produce a revision poster on the content we had taught thus far. For others, I simply wrote out questions on the board for them to answer from a textbook. By all accounts, this does not fit with the requirements of a 'good lesson'. However, in the situation I would argue the opposite. It is about damage limitation. In this situation I aim for;

1) The class to be calm.
2) The class to complete some form of 'work'.

That in itself can be classed as a victory. Poor planning can lead to very poor behaviour, but it does not directly cause it. It is important in this type of situation for the pupils not to suspect that something is majorly wrong. You may want to admit that your computer is broken, but I would advise commenting that you were going to do this lesson at some point anyway. This ensures your classroom routines are not destroyed.

To summarise the learnings of this chapter:
You can and can't control:

1) Extreme scenarios can be hilarious when controlled.
2) Fights are rare. Try and identify pre-cursers.
3) Forgetting your kit is embarrassing. Do what you can to maintain routine and expectations.

CONCLUDING THOUGHTS

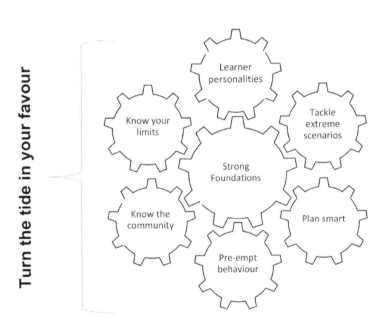

Turn the tide in your favour

Learner personalities

Know your limits

Tackle extreme scenarios

Strong Foundations

Know the community

Plan smart

Pre-empt behaviour

Throughout this guide my aim has been to breakdown my experiences into seven key areas. The 'steadfast 7' should not be viewed in isolation. Instead, I view each of them as a cog within a greater structure. Strong foundations are the core function, which allow the rest to move freely. Without the foundations in place, it is difficult to pre-empt behaviour, or use knowledge of the community to your advantage. If each of the methods are deployed successfully, the system will flow smoothly. The better you manage different learner personalities and the pre-empting of behaviour, the easier it will be for you to deal with extreme scenarios. The 7 strategies for survival will not completely eliminate the challenge that you face in schools. When I first started, at times, I felt overwhelmed by the problems I faced on a daily basis. Using each strategy allowed me to begin overcoming them.

When all is considered, it is important not to lose sight of the things you love about your role. At the end of the day, the core function of teaching is for pupils to learn and progress. Having a calm classroom where the pupils listen to you will enable the vast majority of pupils to learn effectively. A classroom with low level disruption, for example, will have the opposite impact regardless of how 'groundbreaking' the activities are.

The methods in this book were chosen as a way to help you succeed in a 'challenging' school. I argue that this, in turn, enables the pupils you teach to succeed. In disadvantaged communities where achievement is traditionally low, being taught by a strong classroom teacher is vital. The more you improve, the better the outcomes for the pupils.

Thank you for reading this guide, I hope there are some strategies you feel would make a real difference in your classroom.

Printed in Great Britain
by Amazon

41643330R00061